Oh, To Be Like Him!

Weekly Devotions for Developing the Attributes of God

Betty Gossell

Oh, To Be Like Him!: Weekly Devotions for Developing the Attributes of God
Copyright © 2023 by Betty Gossell

ISBN: 979-8988147138 (sc)
ISBN: 979-8988147145 (e)

Riverview Press

info@riverview-press.com
www.riverview-press.com

Oh, To Be Like Him!

Weekly Devotions for Developing
the Attributes of God

Betty Gossell

iii

Special Thanks

As much as I enjoy some of the current worship songs, my heart is stirred the most when I hear an old hymn from my childhood. Whether they are hymns of God's love, salvation, majesty or faithfulness, the words fill me with a reverence for God and the desire to be more like him.

Of course, my parents were the first to introduce me to hymns – taking me to church each week and setting Godly examples for me and my siblings. I also remember my paternal grandmother teaching me to play the piano using an old hymnal as my lesson book. And there have been numerous music teachers and professional musicians who have blessed me over the years. I sincerely thank everyone who has had a musical influence on me and my spiritual journey.

Oh, to be like him, oh to be like him!
Blessed redeemer, pure as thou art.
Come in thy sweetness,
come in thy fullness.
Stamp thine own image,
deep on my heart.

Author: Thomas O. Chisholm (1897)

Betty Gossell

Introduction

Finding time for Bible study is not always easy with the hectic lives we all live. I know I always have good intentions at the start of a new year, but before a few weeks go by I miss a day here and a day there, and then I feel like it's too hard to get caught up.

The format of these devotionals is very simple—they are structured so that you do one per week. Each will take less than 15 minutes to complete. Of course, if you miss a week, just jump back in wherever you want. The devotions include a scripture, a short reflection, a prayer and then there is room to leave your thoughts.

Additionally, they do not have to be read in any special order—if you are dealing with a particular struggle, feel free to skip ahead to whichever reading would be the most beneficial. There are no rules here—use these in the way that is best for you.

My prayer is that you find these reflections to be helpful and that they spur some introspection. I can only hope they bless you as much to read as they did me to write.

Betty Gossell

Table of Contents

CHAPTER 1

Oh, To Be Like Him

Today's Scripture: Genesis 1:27 "So
God created mankind in his own image,
in the image of God he created them;
male and female he created them."

Reflection: As I get older, I realize that what I want
most is to exhibit God in this world, so others can see
him through me. But what does this really mean, and
how would I accomplish it? First, I need to study who
God really is, and what his characteristics are. While
we can never attain his holiness or his infinite power,
we can strive to match his love, kindness, faithfulness,
mercy, and grace towards those around us. By reading
and studying his word, we will see his attributes and
find guidance to developing those traits. Extensive
passages in the Bible are devoted to developing true
love for others, exhibiting mercy and grace, forgiveness, and patience. Look for these verses, memorize
them, and put them into practice. Ask God daily for

help in areas where you are weak – is it holding a grudge? Feeling envious? Battling anger or anxiety? The Bible is full of examples of God's character that we can model ourselves after.

Another help is in learning from others. Whether from sermons at church or group Bible studies, listening to others who can share their experiences and offer suggestions will help us grow more into the image of God. We are blessed to have a wealth of knowledge and inspiration at our fingertips – we can listen to sermons from around the world and from famous speakers from the past. The instructions for reflective living are all around us and we have no excuse not to use them.

Prayer: Oh, God, the desire of my heart is to reflect you into our troubled world. Help me to practice each day the skills I need to develop, and to seek wisdom from others who can guide me on my way to a life in your image. Amen.

Application:

_____

_____

_____

_____

_____

_____

CHAPTER 2

God of Hope

Today's Scripture: Romans 15:13
"May the God of hope fill you with
all joy and peace as you trust in him,
so that you may overflow with hope
by the power of the Holy Spirit."

Reflection: My paternal grandmother Hattie was an amazing woman. She lived a very hard life on a farm with no running water and only a woodburning stove for heat until she was in her 80's. She was a small woman – probably around 5 feet tall – but I rarely ever saw her just sitting and doing nothing. From the day she married my grandfather, she was busy from before dawn until way after sunset: working in the garden, cooking, or cleaning, helping my grandfather with chores, and later taking care of their two children (my dad and his sister Leora.) Tragedy struck the family when Leora died at age 17 from pneumonia after a very short illness.

3

In going through some of her old things, I learned that my grandmother struggled for many years after Leora's death, but eventually she found acceptance and peace. My grandfather died just after his 90th birthday, and Hattie lived another seven years in a retirement center. I never once heard her complain or wish that her life had been different. She continued to read her Bible, prayed for me and was a comfort to me when I was going through challenges of my own. Her quiet voice was warm with encouragement and faith that God would carry me through my dark times, just as he had for her. She never lost her joy or peace, and set such a good example for me, right up until she went to heaven at age 93.

Prayer: Lord, thank you for the Godly example of our ancestors. Thank you for Hattie and all she taught me about faith and love and joy. Help me to be that kind of example to others. Amen.

Application:

_____
_____
_____
_____
_____
_____

CHAPTER 3

A Pure Heart

Today's Scripture: I Timothy 1:5
"The aim of our charge is love that
issues from a pure heart and a good
conscience and a sincere faith."

Reflection: Social media is a fun way to stay in contact with friends and family, to follow celebrities, and share cat videos or pictures of food. But what has crept in with it is the desire to only show the good pictures, in just the right lighting, and with filters to soften the wrinkles or sagging chins. We see photos of gorgeous homes or vacations and perfectly behaving children. Everyone is smiling and having a great time. But pictures are cropped to hide the dishes in the sink or the pile of laundry to be folded. Multiple shots at various angles are taken with only the perfect ones shared online. This need to appear perfect has caused an increase in cyberbullying, social anxiety, and the fear of not measuring up.

When someone looks at me, I want them to see God's love shining through me. I don't want any artificial filters or areas of my life cropped out or hidden. I believe that people respond to a pure heart that points them in the way of faith in God and his promises. My flaws are part of who I am and show that God is patient and kind and forgiving. The world needs plain speech and honest conversation, not the appearance of superiority in my faith or a haughty attitude.

Prayer: Dear Father, your love is perfect and pure. Create in me a pure heart, one that is open and sincere and not clouded by phony words or a pious attitude. Help your love flow through me and into the world around me. My desire is to love like you, every day. Amen.

Reflection:

_____

_____

_____

_____

_____

_____

CHAPTER 4

John 3:16

Today's Scripture: John 3:16 "For
God so loved the world, that he
gave his only begotten Son, that
whosoever believeth in him should not
perish but have everlasting life."

Reflection: This is probably the most famous verse in the Bible, and one of the first you memorized as a child. Outside of church, you have likely seen it on billboards or on signs at a football game. These are such familiar words, but what do they truly mean?

I was fortunate to grow up in a home with two loving Christian parents. I heard from an early age about God and his love, but I hadn't made the connection between "God so loved the world" and "God loves ME." When I was about 12 years old, we had special services at our church that were led by two amazing women - one preached the sermons while the other did chalk drawings. One evening the sermon was about sin and I became convicted about the things I had done wrong in my life and some poor attitudes I had. But then the speaker explained about God's love - not just for the world as a whole but for ME! Even if I was the only person on earth Jesus would have died on the cross, just for me! I was overwhelmed with a mixture of gratitude and unworthiness. I went to the altar and after confessing my sins, I asked Jesus to live in my heart and fill me with his love. That was more than 50 years ago but, in my mind, I can still see that tiny country church and feel my knees on the wooden floor. But more than anything, I can feel God's love around me, welcoming me into a personal relationship with him.

Prayer: Dear Father, thank you for loving me. Even on my best days I am unworthy of such sacrificial love. Help me to live a life worthy of your love for me, and to share that love with the world around me. Amen.

Application:

_____
_____
_____
_____
_____
_____

CHAPTER 5

House on the Rock

Today's Scripture: Matthew 7:24-25
"Therefore everyone who hears these words
of mine and puts them into practice is like
a wise man who built his house on the
rock. The rain came down, the streams
rose, and the winds blew and beat against
that house; yet it did not fall, because
it had its foundation on the rock."

Reflection: One of my favorite memories of our
farm in Iowa was the creek that ran alongside it. We
played on the bank, waded in the water, even ice
skated in the winter (after spending hours clearing
the snow from the ice.) We had been told the creek
had not flooded in at least 50 years, and for the first
six years or so that we lived there, it didn't. Oh, the
water got high sometimes, and even got on the yard
once or twice, but never really came over the banks.
That is until the summer I was 10 years old. Our

house sat back from the edge of the creek a ways, and on one cloudy summer day we suddenly had over 12 inches of water running in the front door and out the back. Almost as quickly as the water rose, we were surrounded by church friends and neighbors who came to help move furniture, sweep and clean the mess, make sure our barn animals were safe, and care for us with food and drinks. The water started to recede before sunset, but mom and dad insisted on all of us kids sleeping elsewhere. I quickly packed an overnight bag and was shuttled off to the home of a friend from 4H. My siblings went to other friends' homes, but mom and dad stayed at our house in case the water came back up. I doubt they slept at all that night. The next week was spent cleaning and scrubbing the dirty water away that had been in almost every room. We were very fortunate that there was no major structural damage and after lots of scrubbing, was inhabitable again. However, 10 days later it flooded again – this time 18 inches deep and covering the electrical outlets in every room. My mother was so exhausted, I remember her sitting in the middle of the kitchen, sobbing. Once again, friends came and helped carry the burden of cleaning and putting our home back together. We were blessed not once but twice within two weeks by people who genuinely loved and cared for us. Our family was built on the rock of Christian friendships.

Prayer: Thank you, Lord, that my childhood home was built on the solid rock of faith and friendship.

You protected us from harm and provided the care and help we needed that summer. Thank you for guiding our steps and keeping us safe during a very challenging time. Help me to be the type of friend who reaches out to others in their time of need, just as those friends did for us so many years ago. Amen.

Application:

_____
_____
_____
_____
_____
_____

CHAPTER 6

Encourage

Today's Scripture: 1 Thessalonians 5:11
"Therefore encourage one another and build
each other up, just as in fact you are doing."

Reflection: I have always loved singing, even from a very early age. I sang in the school choir, in a select girls' group, and was also in a bicentennial musical in 1976. In the 2nd grade our beloved music teacher Miss M pulled me aside one day and said she wanted to start teaching me how to sing harmony. She encouraged me to keep practicing, and in the 3rd grade I was selected to sing a duet in our high school musical "Music Man," even though I was very young and very nervous. Miss M was admired by all her students, and her infectious laugh and caring nature won over the hearts of even the most stubborn teenager. She truly cared about each of us and let us know how important we were to her. I had the opportunity to speak with her a few years ago, not long before she passed away from cancer. She had the same infectious laugh and twinkle in her eyes, and we talked and shared precious memories. I'm not sure any of my teachers had a bigger impact on my life than she did.

How wonderful it is to have people who care for us and encourage us to try new things, or to calm our fears. But can we say we do the same for others? Do we reach out to the lonely or those who are afraid of the future? Are we using our talents and skills to help others reach their potential? Do we take the time to share with others a kind word or encouraging message?

Prayer: Dear Heavenly Father, thank you for the encouragers you send into our lives. Help us in turn to encourage others that we meet throughout the day. Give us more of your compassion and love. Amen.

Application:

_____

_____

_____

_____

_____

_____

CHAPTER 7

Answer Me

Today's Scripture: Psalm 17:6-8 "I call
on you, my God, for you will answer me;
turn your ear to me and hear my prayer.
Show me the wonders of your great love,
you who save by your right hand those
who take refuge in you from their foes.
Keep me as the apple of your eye; hide
me in the shadow of your wings."

Reflection: I grew up in an age before cell phones or
even call waiting and answering machines. In fact,
the farm where I lived as a child had only one phone
that was on a party line. This phone was not for long
conversations with friends but rather for quick messages or emergencies. Even after we moved to town
and had two phones (one upstairs and one down) we
still were to only use it for a few minutes at a time.
Nothing would frustrate one of my parents more than
for them to try to call home and get a busy signal!

I remember a time when I was about 20 years old and had car trouble. I walked to a pay phone (another thing we don't see anymore) and tried to call my dad. Over and over I called, only to get a busy signal. It was cold and snowy and getting dark. I was stranded quite far from my apartment and had no idea what else to do. I could not imagine what was going on at home for the phone to be busy for so long. Finally, I was able to get through, and found out that somehow the phone at home had not been hung up properly and was off the hook. I was so relieved when my dad finally answered and then came to help me!

Isn't it great to know that God is always there to answer when we call? There are no busy signals, no phones left off the hook, no leaving a message at the beep for him to get back to us later. We are not left alone and stranded when we need him the most. And this line is NOT just for emergencies! He actually wants to talk to us and for us to share all parts of our lives with him, both the bad and the good. This line of communication is to work both ways as we talk with him and are in tune with him enough to hear his responses.

Prayer: Thank you, Father, that I always have an open and direct line to you, and that you are never too busy to hear me when I call. Help me to be more comfortable talking to you all throughout my day, and not just when I am in trouble. Amen.

Application:

_____

_____

_____

_____

_____

_____

CHAPTER 8

Next Steps

Today's Scripture: Proverbs 16:9
"We can make our plans, but the
LORD determines our steps."

Reflection: By the end of my junior year in high school, I was feeling pressured to pick a career and select colleges to apply to. I honestly had no idea what I wanted to do with my life – I had lots of things I knew I DIDN'T want to do, but to decide on one thing for the rest of my life? The thought frightened me. My parents did not understand my confusion: both had decided early in life what their futures would look like and had never wavered from those desires. I had spent a lot of high school taking business-related courses such as typing, shorthand and bookkeeping, so I figured I would go to a business school and then… I had no idea. One day I thought about a cousin I admired who was a court reporter. I wrote her a long letter asking lots of questions, and she replied how much she enjoyed her job. It sounded impressive and like something I figured I could do. I did not do as much research about the job as I should have, and certainly didn't pray about it much. But having an answer to the career question got everyone off my back for a while, and that's what mattered most to me at that time.

For about a year I studied court reporting at a business school in Des Moines – most of that time was spent in tears and frustration because it turned out to be NOT the right career for me. As hard as it was for me to admit defeat, I left college and tried to come up with a different plan. Nothing seemed to work, though, and my efforts at forcing myself into career molds that others picked out for me were a dismal failure.

Several years later and after many failed attempts and doors being shut in my face, God finally led me into the job that would evolve into the career of my dreams. When the timing was right and I was ready, this profession was presented to me. God directed me toward the right people and places, and he aligned the timing so that this special opportunity was available just when I needed it. Once I opened my eyes and heart to the path God wanted me to take, I achieved more success and fulfillment than I ever imagined.

Prayer: Lord, thank you that you can take even my best plans and turn them into something better – the place where I needed to be that I never would have found on my own. Thank you for closing the doors that needed to be closed, and opening the ones that revealed your plans for me. Help me to be more receptive to your ways and not try to do everything on my own. Amen.

Application:

_____

_____

_____

_____

_____

_____

CHAPTER 9

I Will Sing

Today's Scripture: Psalm 59:16 "In the morning I will sing of your love."

Reflection: I remember as a little girl waking up early on spring mornings to the intoxicating fragrance of Lily of the Valley flowers. My parents had a small flower garden outside my bedroom. I loved sleeping with my window open a tiny bit, and if the breeze was just right, the dainty scent could slip into my room as the sun was rising. When I peeked outside, I could see dew glistening on the tiny white bells that covered delicate green stalks. My mother also had a bird house in the flower bed that was specifically for wrens (her favorite birds). One morning I awoke to the excited chirping of a pair of wrens and the delicious scent of the lilies floating on the gentle spring breeze. I laid in my bed and took it all in – and marveled at the variety of nature that was waking up with me this new day. Soon I was able to recognize other birds and then sounds of the farm animals or our dog barking. I could hear my parents talking softly at the other end of the house – mom cooking breakfast and dad preparing to go to work. I heard a train off in the distance and an occasional car that rattled across the bridge over the creek that ran beside our farm. My cat hopped onto my bed and then up onto the windowsill where he could keep an eye on the birds flying back and forth. The sights, the sounds, the smells of an early Iowa spring morning - not much was better.

In today's verse, David tells of singing to God in the morning. We have so much to sing about and to be thankful for! We are to sing not just for the beauty of nature, but also in thanks for his love and care for us.

Prayer: Lord, I am in awe of all that you have created, and the amazing variety of sights and sounds and scents you provide for us. All of nature sings to you - help me to see your beauty each day, and to share your love with others. Amen.

Application:

_____

_____

_____

_____

_____

_____

CHAPTER 10

Live in Peace

Today's Scripture: Hebrews 12:14
"Make every effort to live in peace
with everyone and to be holy; without
holiness no one will see the Lord."

Reflection: I was huddled in the corner of an overly crowded storm shelter while tornado sirens blared. There was a confirmed tornado just a few miles from my house and headed my way. The shelter was cramped and claustrophobic. Children were crying and several men were trying to follow the news on their cell phones but unable to get a good signal from our underground shelter. It was dark and damp and scary, but most everyone was concerned for those around them and helping to calm the nerves of those who were afraid. After about 30 minutes, the sirens stopped and one of the men left the shelter to check the news. He learned that the bad weather had moved further east, and that we were going to be safe. We waited a bit longer for the rain to stop, and soon the sun was peeking through the clouds. By the time one of my neighbors walked me home, it was almost impossible to tell how bad the weather had been. A few birds were even chirping in the trees. I was so thankful that I had been with friends and neighbors and not alone, and that we could find peace together in the storm.

God wants us to live in peace with all people, not just those in our family or our close friends. Exhibiting his peace to others is a true reflection of his grace toward me.

Prayer: Dear Father, thank you that we can experience your peace during the storms of life. And thank you for others around us who live lives of peace and harmony with those they know well, and those they had not met before. Amen.

Application:

_____
_____
_____
_____
_____
_____

CHAPTER 11

Be Transformed

Today's Scripture: Romans 12:2 "Do
not conform to the pattern of this world
but be transformed by the renewing of
your mind. Then you will be able to
test and approve what God's will is—
his good, pleasing, and perfect will."

Reflection: I think we all want to feel like we fit in.
I grew up with flaming red hair in a sea of blonds
and brunettes. I started wearing glasses at a very
young age and was teased because of it. I was also
the shortest person in my class. In a world of long-
legged beautiful blonds, I was nowhere near that, and
I remember feeling like an oddball. As a society, we
tend to follow trends in clothing and hairstyles and
types of cars we drive – we have an innate need to
feel part of the group. Fitting in with others seemed
to show we are accepted by the masses.

But does any of that really matter if our hearts
are bitter or our lifestyle is such that it hurts others?

We can have the right brand of shoes or the most popular hairstyle but live a life of hate or anger. Watching the latest hit tv series may give us something to talk about at work tomorrow, but is it a positive message that benefits others? We may spend hours on social media watching dance videos because it is the trending thing to do, but at the end of the day, what kind of impression are we leaving on the world? Do others look at us and see that we are different, not because of what we are wearing or doing, but because of who we are?

God wants to transform us – to make us new creatures that are not part of the current society. We are to be different in how we act, how we dress, or how we talk to each other. We are to stand out from the crowd because of the work he has done in us.

Prayer: Dear Father, help me to not worry about fitting into today's society because of the size of my house or the type of car I drive. Let me see the world through your eyes – the hurting and vulnerable people who need a reflection of you through my words and actions. Transform me into your likeness more and more each day. Amen.

Application:

_____

_____

_____

_____

_____

_____

CHAPTER 12

The Inheritance

Today's Scripture: I Peter 1:3-5 "Praise
be to the God and Father of our Lord
Jesus Christ! In his great mercy he has
given us new birth into a living hope
through the resurrection of Jesus Christ
from the dead, and into an inheritance
that can never perish, spoil or fade. This
inheritance is kept in heaven for you, who
through faith are shielded by God's power
until the coming of the salvation that is
ready to be revealed in the last time."

Reflection: An inheritance is the acquisition of a
possession, condition, or trait from past generations.
Most people think of receiving an inheritance in
monetary terms – houses, land, expensive possessions, and huge checks from insurance proceeds or
savings accounts and investments. Many parents feel
like failures if they do not leave tens of thousands

of dollars to each of their children and/or grandchildren. I've heard of families that almost came to blows because some members felt that others got more money or valuable property in an estate, and they contested the legitimacy of the will. I watched two daughters fight over their mother's furniture, with one of them stealing the drawers from a dresser so her sister could not have it.

My parents were not wealthy people, and when the estate was finalized after mom passed away last year, my siblings and I were able to select a few mementos and we received a small amount of insurance proceeds. However, what I inherited from my parents was far more valuable than any property, possessions, or insurance checks. They modeled for me a work ethic and the values of charity and devotion to family and friends. But more than that, they gave me their examples of trust and faith in God and living a life of honesty and prayer. As special as that is, God has an even greater inheritance for me – a life of peace and love while here on earth and hope of a future in Heaven for eternity. No probate court is needed, no lawyers or accountants are needed. We don't need safety deposit boxes to protect expensive jewelry or security systems for our mansions. The inheritance God has for us can never be taken away.

Prayer: Dear Father, it is so easy for us to get caught up in the values of this world, and to crave possessions more than caring about the inheritance of eternal life you have for us in Heaven. Help me to focus on you and your love for me. Help me to share the great news of this inheritance with others – there is more than enough of your riches to go around! Amen.

Application:

_____
_____
_____
_____
_____
_____

CHAPTER 13

Daily Praise

Today's Scripture: Psalm 145:1-2 "I will praise you, my God and King, and bless your name each day and forever."

Reflection: Going to church camp was a huge part of my life growing up. Whether it was a time for just kids, as a teen or with my family, several weeks each summer were spent at a small campground in southern Iowa. One summer I was a counselor for the kids, spent a week there as a teen, and then went back for 10 days with my family. I knew every square inch of that property, and the memories of the special times I spent there flood my mind. (I even got my first real kiss there!) I made many precious friends there who are still my friends 50+ years later. I have not been there for a long time, but can still describe the sights, the sounds, the feelings of love and excitement and adventure.

I remember one particular summer as a teen when I renewed my commitment to God and was determined to return home a different person, one filled with God's love and with a heart of devotion. I wept at the alter that night, pouring out to God my sins and asking for forgiveness and for his guidance in the days ahead. I was surrounded by my camp friends and several of us bonded together over our experience. I returned home and faithfully read my Bible and prayed each day… well, for a while anyway. Soon it was time to go back to school and my old habits and routines reappeared. While I still was a believer and tried to live my life in a way that was pleasing to God, I was not relying on him for daily help and strength. I stumbled in my faith and fell many times, and I remember being very disappointed in myself. What was missing? It was my daily time with God, talking with him about my struggles and reading his word to learn what he wanted for my life. It is a lesson that I have had to re-learn many times in my adult life. I need a daily infusion of God's word and conversations with him to keep me from wandering astray. I need to praise him each day, thanking him for all he has done for me. I need to stay connected and not feel like I can do things on my own.

Prayer: Thank you, Father, for all that you have done for me over the years. Thank you to the teachers and pastors who influenced me during those early camp experiences and set me on a path to a life living for you. Forgive me for the times I feel I can do 'life' without you. Help me each day to remain faithful to you and to your teachings. Keep me grounded and planted in your word. Amen.

Application:

_____
_____
_____
_____
_____
_____

CHAPTER 14

Lowly

Today's Scripture: Psalm 138:6 "Though the LORD is exalted, he looks kindly on the lowly; though lofty, he sees them from afar."

Reflection: Have you ever felt insignificant or invisible? Have you been in a situation (whether at work or school or church) where you felt no one even noticed you were there? Lowly means "of low status or importance." How many of us have felt that way as children, or now that we are adults?

I am a relatively shy person and tend to hold back when entering new situations. Taking leadership roles at work has been tough for me, but I have gotten a bit better with it over the years. Social situations, however, continue to be difficult and I usually sit on the sidelines until I am more comfortable, or someone reaches out to me first. I never wanted a solo in band or choir – I was perfectly content to provide harmony in the background. The few times that I was 'out front' such as having the lead in the school play or a solo in a musical brought intense feelings of fear and inadequacy. But the innate need to feel seen or heard was still there, as it is for all of us.

Today's verse reminds us that God sees each of us, even those of us in the background. We don't need to be at the front of the stage or the CEO of a business for him to recognize our presence. Even from his 'exalted' position in heaven he is intimately aware of us as individuals and the challenges we face. We are not insignificant or invisible to him – he loves and cares for us all and is willing to meet us wherever we are.

Prayer: Dear Father, thank you for this day and for loving us. Thank you that your attention to us is not based on any earthly status or fame, but that you look kindly toward each of us. Help us to do the same with others we meet throughout our day. Amen.

Application:

_____
_____
_____
_____
_____
_____

CHAPTER 15

Laughter

Today's Scripture: Psalm 47:1 "Clap
your hands, all you nations; shout
to God with cries of joy."

Reflection: Is there anything more beautiful – or contagious - than the laughter of a small child? Something happens to most babies around nine months of age where it seems they discover their 'giggle box' as my mom used to call it, and they find everything hilariously amusing. It is almost impossible to hear their squeals of joy and not join them. Some babies laugh so hard they almost fall over.

I remember when my granddaughter was about this age. I was holding her in my lap and my daughter was making funny faces at her from across the room. Giggles filled the air, and my heart exploded with joy. But there are other times we experience joy with our children – when they learn to walk or talk or are discovering the wonders of nature and creation. The first time they really smell a flower or experience a new food that they love, when they accomplish a task all by themselves or hand you a picture they have colored: there is joy in the discovering, joy in the sharing.

When we think about God and all that he has done for us, what is our emotion? Do we even really think about it much at all? How many of us ever sit back, close our eyes, and let our hearts be filled with pure joy? When someone looks at us, do they see anything in our face that separates us from the crowd? Is there joy in our lives that is bubbling forth like giggles from a toddler, and so contagious the whole room experiences it? I know that it is easy to be caught up in the daily drama of our lives and to not feel overly joyful at times. Life can be hard with sadness and sorrow, fears of the future or grief for what is lost. But God wants our lives to be filled with the joy of his faithfulness to us, and to share that joy with others. Clap your hands – shout for joy – for all he has done for us in the past, and for all he will do for us in the future and throughout eternity.

Prayer: Dear Father, forgive me for the times I do not express my thankfulness and joy to you. You have provided for me more than I could ever deserve, and for that I am grateful. Let the joy of my salvation fill my life and spill over into the lives of others. Amen.

Application:

_____

_____

_____

_____

_____

_____

CHAPTER 16

An Ordinary Girl

Today's Scripture: Acts 4:13 "When they (the Sanhedrin) saw the courage of Peter and John and realized that they were unschooled, ordinary men, they were astonished, and they took note that these men had been with Jesus."

Reflection: It is easy for me to think that I do not have enough religious knowledge to share my faith with others. While I am college-educated and have been in church all my life, I never attended seminary or learned to speak in Greek or Hebrew. I don't know all of the Bible by heart, nor have I spoken to huge crowds or written best-selling religious books. What do I possibly have to share that would be meaningful, or that does not sound superficial or foolish?

Our verse above tells us that Peter and John (Heroes of our Faith) were just ordinary men, but their impact has lasted for over 2000 years because they had been with Jesus. Fancy words and deep theological thinking are not needed to share Jesus with others – we just need a grateful heart and a desire to see others experience God's love and peace in their lives. It's okay that I am just an 'ordinary girl," because I have had Jesus speak to me, love me, and save me. My life is not perfect, but God has answered prayers and moved in mysterious ways for me. I cannot imagine living this life without his guidance or facing eternity without him. That is something that I can share with others.

Prayer: Dear Father, help me not to feel inferior to share my faith, but instead to be bold and confident in what you have given me to speak. Everyone has a story, and each story is important and worthy of hearing. Thank you for loving me, and for giving me opportunities to share that love whenever I can. Amen.

Application:

_____

_____

_____

_____

_____

_____

CHAPTER 17

Care Bears

Today's Scripture: Ephesians 4:32 "Be kind
to one another, tenderhearted, forgiving one
another, as God in Christ forgave you."

Reflection: Many of you will remember the Care
Bears that were popular in the 1980's, and then again
in the 2000's. My daughter Karen was totally in love
with those colorful animals – in fact, her nickname
was KareBear. She had Care Bear toys, clothes, post-
ers, stuffed animals and even sheets for her bed. I
didn't mind indulging her, since the qualities these
cuddly bears exhibited were friendship, being cheerful, loving others and having a tender heart. (Well,
there was also Grumpy Bear, but we are all allowed
to be grumpy once in a while.) What was obvious by
looking at the bears was that they wore their attitudes
on their tummies for all the world to see. There was
no hiding or pretending to be something they were

not. And each one was doing their part to make my child feel happy and loved.

Whether we want to or not, what we 'wear' in our hearts is shared with others. What are you showing the world each day? Are you showing love, friendship, or cheer, and then spreading it to the world? Is your presence comforting to others? Or can everyone tell you are a grumpy bear as soon as you enter the room?

Prayer: Dear God, I want your love, kindness, and tenderness to radiate from me wherever I go, when I talk to someone on the phone, or even when I am stuck in traffic. Help me to exhibit your tender heart to others, and for them to see your reflection in everything I do. Amen.

Reflection:

_____
_____
_____
_____
_____
_____

CHAPTER 18

The Rock

Today's Scripture: Psalm 61:2 "When
my heart is overwhelmed, lead me
to the rock that is higher than I."

Reflection: Except for a few years here and there, I have lived my entire life within a couple of miles of my parents. I saw them several times each week, and on the days I did not see them, we talked on the phone. They were available to help me when I had surgery and I was able to run errands for them or care for them in their later years. I often asked my dad for advice, and my mom was my confidante and best friend. My dad passed away from cancer in 2015, and my mother also succumbed to the disease in 2022. The loss of their presence in my daily life was a huge bottomless pit of sadness and loneliness for me. As crazy as my life was, I knew I could always count on them. And now they are gone.

Some days are more difficult than others, but I doubt a day has gone by when I have not thought of one or both of them. Vacations, working in the garden, making jigsaw puzzles, fishing trips, big family meals and times at church – my parents impacted every part of my life, not just as a child but also as an adult. Some days I get bogged down in my grief and have found the only way out is to look up into the face of God. His strong arms comfort me, his gentle voice calms my fears of the future, and his tender hands wipe away my tears. As a mountain towers over the surrounding countryside, I need God's presence to tower over the grief and sadness in my life.

Prayer: Dear Father, thank you for my parents and other important people in my life. Help me to appreciate those who are still with me, and to remember fondly those who have gone on before. You are my comforter in times of grief, and the strong rock I can cling to when my life is unsettled. Thank you for loving me. Amen.

Application:

_____

_____

_____

_____

_____

_____

CHAPTER 19

Sleep

Today's Scripture: Psalm 4:8 "In peace
I will lie down and sleep, for you alone,
Lord, make me dwell in safety."

Reflection: I have always been very fortunate in that I can fall asleep almost anywhere. My many years of travelling as a healthcare consultant involved two to three flights each week, many of which were delayed or canceled, and I would fly through the night and into the wee hours of the morning. It didn't matter if it was dark where I was or the middle of the day, noisy or quiet, if I was in a comfy bed or sitting in a chair: If I'm tired, I sleep! One particular trip involved an 8 AM flight from Dallas to El Paso, Texas. As we pushed back from the gate, I closed my eyes and was asleep before we even took off. The next thing I knew we had a very rough landing in El Paso, and I was jolted awake. It was 1 ½ hours later – I had slept the whole trip. My seat mate turned to look at me and said, "Wow, you are good! How in the world did you manage to sleep the entire time?" I told him I had been on hundreds of flights and had faith that the pilot and crew would keep me as safe as possible. I had a busy work week ahead of me and might as well rest while I could.

So, falling asleep has never been my problem–but staying asleep? That is something I have struggled with much of my life. Usually after about two or three hours of restful sleep, my brain shifts into overdrive and I toss and turn, worrying about work or money or family or world problems or the weather (especially tornados here in Oklahoma), and before long it is time for the alarm to go off and I am starting another workday, exhausted. Why is it so difficult for me to relax and go back to sleep? Why does this happen night after night?

Our verse today tells us that the Lord supplies rest for us as we dwell in his safety. It is up to me to turn my worries and fears over to him and let him fight my battles while I rest. Psalm 94:19 states, "When anxiety was great within me, your consolation brought me joy." If I want joy and rest and peace, I need to take my hands off my worries and give them over to the One who wants to provide restorative sleep. Refreshment is waiting for me; I just need to accept it.

Prayer: Dear Father, I come to you today exhausted; struggling with my anxieties and worry. Help me to turn these fears over to you and learn to rest in the safety you have promised to provide. Thank you for loving me and caring for me, offering the rest I need. Amen.

Application:

_____

_____

_____

_____

_____

_____

CHAPTER 20

The Letter

Today's Scripture: 2 John 1:12 "Though
I have many things to write to you, I do
not want to do so with paper and ink; but
I hope to come to you and speak face to
face, so that your joy may be made full."

Reflection: I loved writing letters as a child, especially to my grandparents in Minnesota. Letters from them did not come very often and were usually filled with routine details like the weather or how the kittens were doing. Each letter ended with the question, "When are you coming to visit?" How I treasured those words and could imagine their farm with the cats in the barn or the long walk to the outhouse. My grandparents were in their 40's when they got married (something very unusual for the times) and in their late 70's by the time I was born. They passed away a long time ago, but I remember them as two kind and gentle people who wanted little more than to spend time with us grandchildren. I know they treasured my letters, just as I did theirs, but the words paled in comparison to a visit from us. Grandpa would let us help him on the farm, care for the animals or play in the barn. His gentle voice led us in devotions each morning. Grandma was always busy with cooking or cleaning or growing the most beautiful flowers, but when she did take a break, it was often to beat me at a game of Chinese checkers or to play hymns on her old piano, a piano I later inherited. She was quiet, soft-spoken, tender-hearted, and kind. Our letters back and forth were special and something I treasure to this day, but nothing beats the time we were able to spend together in person.

God has written hundreds of letters to us—words of love and faith and forgiveness. The Bible is full of his wisdom, his guidance, and his plans for us. And while we do not mail physical letters to him, he does love to hear from us, both the good and the bad. He wants us to share the details of our lives with him, even how things like the weather affect us, and he wants to listen to our fears and worries. But just imagine what it will be like when we finally get to be together! Not only will our joy be made full, but his as well.

Prayer: Dear Father, how I treasure the letters you have written to me. Your love and kindness pour out on every page. Help me to respond to those words with words of my own—words of faith and trust and gratitude. But more than anything, I long for the day when I can see you face-to-face and express that love in person. What a joyful day that will be! Amen.

Application:

_____

_____

_____

_____

_____

_____

CHAPTER 21

All Things New

Today's Scripture: Revelation 21:5 "He who was seated on the throne said, 'I am making everything new!' Then he said, 'Write this down, for these words are trustworthy and true.'"

Reflection: Have you ever gone back to your childhood home or hometown and found that everything looked entirely different? I had the chance to take a trip with my oldest sister and go back to the farm where we lived as children. Even before we drove down the long driveway, I could tell that so much had changed. There used to be a large garden and a small fenced area where we kept the chickens and my brother's 4H sheep. The old barn was gone, along with a few of the smaller outbuildings. In their place was a beautiful new barn and I had heard that the current owners raised and boarded horses. We stayed in the car but looked at the house from the outside–

the basic shape was the same and the memories came flooding back, but yet it was unfamiliar since many things seemed different. I hadn't expected things to stay the same for 50 years, but the changes unsettled me a bit. Our trip continued with a stop at our old elementary school, which is not a school anymore but was divided into small apartments. Trees were gone, new homes had been built in entirely new subdivisions, and even the rickety old bridge near our farm had been replaced.

I feel like God looks at us much the same way. Not content to leave us as we are, he wants to remove what is no longer beneficial and for us to put away our childish things so he can build us up into new and better lives. He doesn't want us to hang on to habits that are familiar to us but outdated, but rather wants us to find new purpose and ways to serve. Memories (even those of better times) are nice, but we cannot live in the past. God wants to make us new and equip us for service and worship today and into the future.

Prayer: Dear Father, while it is fun to go down memory lane and relive exciting times from our youth, help me stay focused on the future and be willing to let go of the things that are holding me back. Build in me new skills and open fresh doors for me. I want to serve you today and forever. Amen.

Application:

_____

_____

_____

_____

_____

_____

CHAPTER 22

Cry Out

Today's Scripture: Psalm 34:17
"The righteous cry out, and the
LORD hears them; he delivers
them from all their troubles."

Reflection: As a teenager, I loved going to youth camp with my church friends. One summer we were at the lake and were playing with a huge inner tube from a tractor tire. We were seeing how many people we could get to stand up on it before it tipped over. It was tons of fun, and our laughter filled the air each time we toppled over. The more we practiced, the more successful we became. As more teens were able to climb on, the splash was even bigger when we all fell off. One time, however, the tube tipped over and I ended up on the bottom of the pile, face-down in the mud at the bottom of the lake. I was buried under several others and could not get up. Everything was a tangle of legs and arms and soon I was unable to breathe. I started to panic and thrash in the water. The harder I fought to get up, the worse it seemed to get. Suddenly, I felt a strong hand grabbing one of my ankles and dragging me from under the pile. Once I got my head above water, I started gasping for air and spitting out water and mud. When I could breathe again, I realized that it was one of the pastors who had seen me struggling and come to my rescue. How fortunate for me that he was paying attention and not distracted by the other teens in the lake! The ending could have been so very different!

Friend, God so badly wants to rescue us from our problems – both big and small. His eyes are always on us, and he sees our struggles. Call out to him if you can. But even if you cannot find the words, reach out to him and he will pull you from the mud to help you breathe freely again.

Prayer: Dear Father, thank you for all the times you have rescued me, even the times when I was unable to cry out to you. It is amazing to know that you never get distracted, and your eyes are always watching me. Help me to trust that you only want what is best for me. Amen.

Application:

_____

_____

_____

_____

_____

_____

CHAPTER 23

Who Can Know?

Today's Scripture: I Corinthians 2:11 "No one can know a person's thoughts except that person's own spirit, and no one can know God's thoughts except God's own Spirit."

Reflection: Many times in my life I have made assumptions about how someone felt about me, or what their words actually meant. Instead of asking the person directly, I let my emotions and imagination run wild, and my feelings were hurt by perceived negative comments. I let these assumptions cloud future interactions between us. This is even more common now with emails and text messages—it is all too easy to misread the sender's intentions and assume the worst. Without facial expressions and body language, it is easy to get the wrong messages. These messes could easily have been cleared up if I had just asked for clarification.

I think we do the same type of things with God. We misread his lessons for us or jump to conclusions if our prayers are not answered on our timeline. We make assumptions based on past experiences or biases. We harbor hurt feelings and mistrust. But God is the one with full knowledge of our situations and has the answers to our questions. We need to listen more closely to him.

Prayer: Dear Father, help me to seek your wisdom and not jump to conclusions based on my past experiences or emotions. You hold my future in your hands, and I desire to know more about your plans for my life. Speak to me through scripture and the teachings of others. Help me to hear your voice clearly so there are no misunderstandings. Amen.

Application:

_____

_____

_____

_____

_____

_____

CHAPTER 24

Need vs Want

Today's Scripture: Psalm 23:1 "The Lord
is my shepherd; I shall not want."

Reflection: "I want! I want! I want!" Those were the words I often heard from my daughter when she was very young. Any trip to the grocery store or Walmart was met with incessant begging for new toys, snacks, or clothes. I threatened to change her middle name to "I want" because I heard it so often. At least she was being honest and not confusing needs with wants. She had what she needed, but it didn't seem to be enough for her, and her wants were constant and almost overpowering.

Our verse above states that with Jesus as our shepherd, we can choose not to want anything else. Jesus satisfies our needs, and we realize that with him, we need nothing more. He provides salvation, peace, security, safety, and comfort in times of trials. He grants us life and the beauty of nature. He gives us his word so we can learn more about him. He walks beside us, so we are never alone.

Just as we grow in our faith over time and learn to trust more in Jesus, my daughter matured and found that wanting all the 'things' was not what would make her happy in the end. God's gifts are perfect for us, and we are content in knowing that he is the ultimate provider. One of the key names for God is JEHOVAH-JIREH, which means God is our Provider. With him lovingly supplying our needs, we have no reason to want anything more.

Prayer: Dear Father, thank you for being my provider. Help me to recognize the difference between wants and needs, and to be more appreciative of your provision in my life. Amen.

Application:

_____

_____

_____

_____

_____

_____

CHAPTER 25

Be Still

Today's Scripture: Exodus 14:14
"The LORD will fight for you;
you need only to be still."

Reflection: How many times have you watched a child struggle with a difficult task, and they refuse to ask for help? You want to help them – you know it is something far beyond their age or capabilities, but they resist any attempt you make to provide even a little bit of assistance. Everyone's stress level rises, and it usually ends in a meltdown of some sort. I remember when I was trying to learn how to ride a bike. My older siblings seemed to learn quite easily, but I really struggled. I was very small for my age (I was usually the shortest person in my class at school) but the smallest bike my parents had was too tall for me. I insisted on trying to ride anyway, but it always ended in scraped knees and elbows, and lots of teasing and laughter from my older brother. I was so stubborn - I tried over, and over, and over, but the results were always the same. After patching up my knees (and pride) for the umpteenth time, my mom finally asked my dad to get some training wheels for me. Dad wasn't a fan of that at first, but finally relented and put them on for me. What a difference! I gained the confidence to ride and have fun with my siblings while I waited for my little legs to grow a bit longer. When we finally took the training wheels off, I was ready to go on long bike rides to the country store with my family. I wish I had asked for help sooner—it would have saved a lot of pain and scars on my knees!

God wants us to stop struggling on our own power and turn the difficult tasks over to him. There is a popular saying "Let Go and Let God," and I think it applies here. I don't know why we find it so hard to give the control of our situations over to God – he is all-knowing and all-powerful. Of course he can fight our battles for us! This is a verse I plan to memorize and reflect on each day.

Prayer: Thank you, God, for having the answers to my struggles if I will just let go and give control to you. Help me to surrender to you daily and not as a last resort because I have tried it on my own and skinned my knees. Amen.

Application:

_____

_____

_____

_____

_____

_____

CHAPTER 26

God is Our Guide

Today's Scripture: Psalm 48:14 "For this God is our God for ever and ever; He will be our guide even unto death."

Reflection: In the early 2000's, I was living and working near the coast in central California. One Saturday afternoon I decided to go exploring, so without much in the way of directions, I planned to drive east toward the central valley. How complicated could it be? I would drive around for a while, take a few pictures, and head back home before dark. Little did I know that there is a phenomenon known as tule fog, which Wikipedia describes as "a thick ground fog that settles in the San Joaquin Valley and Sacramento Valley areas of California's Central Valley... Visibility in tule fog is usually less than an eighth of a mile (about 600 ft). Visibility can vary rapidly; in only a few feet, visibility can go from 10 feet to near zero."

And zero visibility it was! I had no idea where I was and was totally encased in unbelievably thick fog. I crept along on what I thought was the right highway at about 5 miles per hour for what seemed like ages, my hands gripping the wheel and so worried I would run off the road or be hit by someone. Suddenly, off to my right I could barely see the sign for a Best Western hotel, almost invisible in the thick fog. I went inside and begged for a room – any room – and luckily, they had a vacancy. But I would have slept in my car if I had to – I was just so glad to be off the road. The fog didn't lift until close to noon the next morning, and then I was able to drive the rest of the way home safely.

God truly had his hand on me that night. I had no business being out alone in unfamiliar territory without a map or other directions. God guided my car and led me to the hotel – I am confident in that. But God wants to be our guide in other times as well, not just the life-threatening ones. Whatever the circumstances, I can be confident that God will be with me, guiding me, if I let him take control of the steering wheel, and my life.

Prayer: Dear Father, thank you for being with me that night, and all the other nights when I am lost or afraid. You know the road before me, and the best way out of the messes I make. Help me to listen to your voice of guidance and to follow your lead. Amen.

Application:

_____

_____

_____

_____

_____

_____

CHAPTER 27

Soaring

Today's Scripture: Isaiah 40:31 "But they that wait upon the Lord shall renew their strength; they shall mount up with wings as eagles; they shall run, and not be weary; and they shall walk, and not faint."

Reflection: I think we all have times in our lives when things are going well – we have a good job, satisfying relationships, and happy/healthy kids and grandkids. God is blessing us, and we feel that we are soaring through life. Small issues come up from time to time, but we cheerfully attack them, and we continue on. Other times, things are a bit challenging – a child is acting out at school or there is stress at work. But God's faithfulness helps us to keep running the good race.

But I doubt there is a person alive who hasn't experienced a time when everything was falling apart. Health, job, finances, family, or even a natural disaster – not an area of your life is unaffected. It's like the old saying, "When it rains, it pours!" Sometimes it is so hard to even put one foot in front of the other, and we may even fall on our knees and attempt to crawl across the rocky ground of our life. But those are the times we need God the most, and we rely not on our own strength but God's to help us through our most difficult days.

I recently experienced a time of struggle in many areas of my life. I had financial worries, family stress and illness, health concerns of my own and a loss of my job – all at the same time. Each burden on its own was challenging enough but adding them together felt like I was being crushed under the weight of it all. In my desperation, I called out to God, and I felt his loving arms around me – lifting me up, helping me to take things one step at a time. I was close to fainting, but God was there to help me. And he will help you, too, if you ask him.

Prayer: Dear God, thank you that I don't have to try to navigate the trials of life on my own. Help me to make spending time with you in your word and memorizing scripture more of a priority, along with turning my struggles over to you for resolution. When things are going well, help me to praise you. And when things are difficult and all my strength is gone, come and lift me up so I can continue to walk with you. Amen.

Application:

_____

_____

_____

_____

_____

_____

CHAPTER 28

The Gift

Today's Scripture: I Peter 4:10 "As each
one has received a special gift, employ it
in serving one another as good stewards
of the manifold grace of God."

Reflection: I have a few vivid memories of my early
childhood, and one special time was my 3rd birthday. My parents had 5 children within 8 years of mar-
riage, and money was often tight. As the 3rd girl in
the family, I had mostly hand-me-down clothes and
very few new toys. But on my 3rd birthday I remember opening a present that was a brand-new doll. She
was wearing a blue satin dress with lots of lace, and
she had blond hair and blue eyes. She even had that
'new doll smell'—I thought she was the most beautiful doll I had ever seen. The only other thing I really
remember of that day was that I wanted to share my
present with a friend who lived across the street. The
town where we lived at the time was quite small and

my mom stood on the front steps and watched as I crossed the street and knocked on my friend's door. My 3-year-old heart was so excited and knew that this gift needed to be shared.

As the years have passed, I have received many more gifts – some from family and friends, and many from God. I have come to recognize God's gifts in my life, and I need to do more than just acknowledge them or use them when or how I see fit. Whether tangible gifts of creativity and music, or emotional gifts of empathy and compassion, God expects me to not only be excited about them, but to enthusiastically rush to share the good news of salvation and his love with others. I am to use my gifts to further his kingdom, and to cultivate relationships with others that develop because of them.

Prayer: Dear Heavenly Father, thank you for all the gifts you have given me over the years. You have lavished favors on me – both big and small – and I am so appreciative. Help me to be even more excited about these gifts, and to develop them further to share with others. Amen.

Application:

_____

_____

_____

_____

_____

_____

CHAPTER 29

A Life of Plenty

Today's Scripture: Isaiah 53:11 "And
the Lord will continually guide you and
satisfy your desire in scorched places and
give strength to your bones. And you will
be like a watered garden, like a spring
of water whose waters do not fail."

Reflection: My mother was born in 1931, in the middle of the Great Depression. She told me many stories about their difficulties during that time, but none was harder than when her mother was diagnosed with tuberculosis and sent away to a sanitorium for several years. My grandfather was without a steady job and was now faced with raising a young child alone. My mother was sent to live with her grandmother, and grandpa went from town to town looking for work. Even once my grandmother recovered and returned home, times were tough and there was the nagging worry of where their next meal would come from. Work was scarce, money was limited, and fears about the future were real.

My parents were married in the early 50's, and throughout their time together there were lean times and times of 'enough.' Both were very hard workers, always trying to provide for their growing family. But my mom never totally relaxed. She lived to the age of 91, and I'm not sure she ever really lost that fear of food insecurity.

In the verses above, we are told that God will provide for us and give us strength even when times are tough – we just need to trust him. Instead of the parched dust bowl of the 30's, he wants our lives to be like a lush garden with running waters nearby. He wants to save us from the heat and despair of the scorched countryside and deliver us to lands of plenty.

Prayer: Dear Father, thank you for your provisions for me. Whether in times of plenty or times of need, I know I can trust you to provide for me and help me through the tough times. Amen.

Application:

_____
_____
_____
_____
_____
_____

CHAPTER 30

Let Love Never Leave

Today's Scripture: Hebrews 12:14
"Make every effort to live in peace
with everyone and to be holy; without
holiness no one will see the Lord."

Reflection: I have never liked conflict. As a middle child, I often found myself as a referee between my siblings, trying to smooth troubled waters and mend broken fences. In a large family, there were always going to be differing opinions on how things should be done, when, and by whom. I don't thrive in situations dominated by chaos, so it has always been my goal for those around me to live and work in harmony. Sometimes it takes sacrifice and hard work, but the results are always worth it.

Our verse today instructs us to make living in peace with others a priority. Are we going out of our way to be courteous to others, even if we feel they are in the wrong? Do we make the effort to really listen to others, speak kindly and then react slowly? Are we putting the needs of friends and family ahead of our own whenever possible? Living in peace with others IS possible, but it takes real effort.

Prayer: Dear Father, it's not always easy to live in peace with others, especially when strong opinions and behaviors are involved. Help me to really listen to others and to seek ways to diffuse difficult situations and conversations. Let your peace shine through me and to be a light in our troubled world. Amen.

Application:

_____

_____

_____

_____

_____

_____

CHAPTER 31

Passwords

Today's Scripture: Psalm 89:15
"Blessed are the people who know
the passwords of praise…" (MSG)

Reflection: "You have exceeded the limit of password attempts and your account has now been locked." I was trying to sign in to a retirement account that I had not used in a while, and I was sure that I remembered the password. My three tries were unsuccessful, and now I could not make the fund transfer that I wanted. It took several phone calls and much time spent on hold before I was able to set up new access. Finally, I was able to complete my business, but I was frustrated and tired, and angry that I had wasted so much time. How much easier this task would have been if I had just used the correct password at the start.

I look at my regular daily activities much the same way. Starting my day off without time spent with God, praising and worshiping him, is like trying to use a computer program without the correct password. Focusing on him and his plan for my life is so much more beneficial than struggling to do things on my own, and usually making things worse. Errors and frustrations can be avoided (or at least decreased) by starting my day in praise for his love for me.

Prayer: Dear Father, help me to use the correct passwords at the start of each day – passwords of praise and thanksgiving, faith, and devotion, and allow you to open the doors and windows that are best for me each day. Help me to put you first in my life. Amen.

Application:

_____

_____

_____

_____

_____

_____

CHAPTER 32

Sweet Friendship

Today's Scripture: Psalm 27: 9 "A
sweet friendship refreshes the soul."

Reflection: I met Karen H over 50 years ago at
church camp in Iowa. She was a few years older than
me, but I liked her a lot. I spent time with her each
summer until I moved away at age 20. We came in
contact again several years later after I moved back
to the area and her father became the pastor of my
church. Both young single mothers, we developed a
rich and strong friendship. Her son and my daughter were true besties, and since their birthdays were
within a week of each other, we often had joint par-
ties. A few years later I moved to Oklahoma, and she
got remarried, but we stayed in touch and remained
friends. She did not have a sister, so selected me to be
an honorary one; a position I gladly accepted. Karen
was always very strong in her faith and was often a

great encourager to me. She was quick to praise and slow to find fault. She was always so supportive of my writings, and the first to ask when a new book would be finished. I can only pray that I was as good a friend to her as she was to me.

Friendship is a precious thing we should never take for granted. I found out yesterday that Karen passed away a few days ago after a sudden illness. My heart is crushed with grief, but yet it smiles at the fond memories of movies and pizza and watching Iowa Hawkeye basketball games together on TV. Her friendship truly refreshed my soul.

Prayer: Thank you, Father, for friends here on earth– friends like Karen and others who have blessed me over the years with their kindness and prayers. I know that she is with you, God, reunited with her family and out of pain. Help me to be a friend to others and spread your love the way Karen did with me. Amen.

Application:

_____
_____
_____
_____
_____
_____

CHAPTER 33

No Longer Lost

Today's Scripture: Ezekiel 34:16 "I will search for my lost ones who strayed away, and I will bring them safely home again."

Reflection: Growing up on a farm in Iowa, I was always surrounded by animals: dogs, cats, cows, chickens, pigs, sheep, horses and an occasional goose or two. I spent many hours playing with and taking care of those animals, but by far my favorite pet was my black and white cat Spotty. He was a great cat, full of snuggles and purrs. He loved being on my lap while I was sitting under a tree watching the birds and squirrels, or just napping in the sun. He was infinitely patient with me when I dressed him in doll clothes, and always came running when I called.

One afternoon I went out to play with him and could not find him. I called his name over and over but got no response. The other half-dozen cats we had came rushing toward me, but not him. I looked in the barn, along the creek and even in the garage, but he was nowhere to be found. I started to worry– had he wandered off and gotten hit by a car? Did he get stepped on by a cow or horse? Had he fallen in the creek? My mother tried to comfort me by saying he had probably gone to a neighboring farm to visit his girlfriend, but I was devastated and feared he would never come home. He was gone for several days, and it even stormed one night. I was losing hope in finding him.

My two older sisters left shortly after supper one night to ride their bikes about a mile to their piano lessons. Our property was situated such that the farm was bordered by a small creek with a railroad on the other side and then a dirt road. As my sisters were on their way home, they heard a loud 'meow' from the ditch, and there was Spotty! He was a bit wet and dirty, but happy to see them. My sisters yelled out to me (I could see them from across the small creek) and told me they found him! I was so excited! He followed my sisters home and trotted down the driveway toward me! He jumped into my arms, and I covered him with kisses and hugs. I never wanted him out of my sight again!

This story makes me think of God's love for us, and how sad he is when we wander astray. Each one of us is precious to him – he never stops looking for us and calling for us to come home. No matter what kind of trouble we may have gotten into, he welcomes us home and takes us into his arms.

Prayer: Dear Father, oh, how much you love us and want us to be with you! You search for us, call to us, and never give up wanting us by your side. Please help me to hear you when you call, and to rush back to you to stay with you forever. Amen.

Application:

_____

_____

_____

_____

_____

_____

CHAPTER 34

It Is Good

Today's Scripture: Proverbs 31:18 "She perceives that her merchandise is good, and her lamp does not go out by night."

Reflection: My mom sewed a lot when I was younger and made many of my clothes. I remember being fascinated that she could lay out some fabric, mark off some measurements, and then soon I would have a dress or shirt. Once she made a cute corduroy jumper for me that was printed with cats, and even had enough left over to make a matching dress for one of my dolls. As a working mother living on a farm and caring for a husband and five children, she often had to work late into the night to get her projects completed. Once I was older, she taught me some sewing basics which I developed further in 4H and then by taking sewing classes in high school. There was a lot of trial-and-error, and the seam ripper was my best friend. I made many of my own things, but really put my machine to use once my daughter was born. I loved sewing for her, and one time I stayed up almost all night to make a formal that she told me she needed at the last minute. Sure, I was tired the next day, but there was a great sense of pride in making something special and one-of-a-kind. My sewing was not limited to just clothing - I went on to make home décor items like pillows, curtains and even a bed spread.

Our verse above describes the woman from Proverbs 31 who has started a side business to supplement the family income. She has already done everything to keep her family fed and well cared for, but she is using her gift as a weaver and seamstress and making items that could be sold across the region to benefit others. She has spent many years perfecting her craft, and now is able to reap the rewards.

What is your gift that inspires you to work late into the night? It may be painting, or writing, or sewing. God has given you many gifts – are you using them for his glory?

Prayer: Dear Father, thank you for the gifts you have given me. Help me to practice and develop them into what you want them to be. Lead me to opportunities to share this gift with others. Amen.

Application:

_____

_____

_____

_____

_____

_____

CHAPTER 35

Perfect Peace

Today's Scripture: Isaiah 26:3 "You will keep in perfect peace those whose minds are steadfast, because they trust in you."

Reflection: My dad grew up in northern Minnesota and loved fishing on several of the 10,000 lakes. Many of our family vacations when I was young were trips to visit my grandparents and then spending time 'drowning a few worms' as my mother would call it. We also made a few fishing trips into Canada, and I loved the wild scenery and remote locations. I enjoyed fishing with my dad and have many precious memories of our time together.

Dad's favorite way to fish was using a trolling motor and we would chug our way slowly across the lake, each of us with a pole and shiny lure temping the fish to bite. I would close my eyes and feel the warm sun on my body and the gently rocking of the boat. I could hear the water lapping against the sides and an occasional songbird or frog. Once I had nearly drifted off to sleep when my line was jerked hard by a nice-sized fish, and I almost lost hold of my pole! I was happy and content that day – fully at peace. After a while, however, it got rather windy, and the water was very choppy. But I had faith in my dad that we would make it safely back to shore, and we did.

God wants to give us his peace, whether our situation is calm and beautiful or if the water is a bit choppy and the ride is stressful. Peace is easy on the pretty days, but when the winds blow and navigation is more difficult, we can rest in his peace then, too, because of our faith.

Prayer: Dear God, help me to rest in the peace you provide to me through faith in you. Whether it is smooth sailing, or I am caught in a storm, I know I can trust in you to deliver me safely home. Thank you for your love. Amen.

Application:

_____
_____
_____
_____
_____
_____

CHAPTER 36

Old Age

Today's Scripture: Isaiah 46:4 "I will be
your God throughout your lifetime—
until your hair is white with age. I
made you, and I will care for you. I
will carry you along and save you."

Reflection: As a child and through my teen years,
I attended a tiny country church in rural Iowa. The
average weekly attendance ranged from about 40 to
maybe 80 on a special Sunday. Among this small
group was a very special man named Russell, who
was about the age of my grandfathers (one of whom
died when I was almost five and the other just before
I turned 10.) Russell was a lovely, kind, and gentle
man, and before long I had developed a friendship
and relationship with him as he took on a grandfa-
therly role in my life. I loved listening to him talk,
pray, and sing. He was hard working and cared faithfully for his wife and family. One week my Sunday

School class was challenged to 'adopt a grandma or grandpa' and I made sure I got to Russell first before any of my friends could grab him. We all went out to lunch at a nice restaurant, and I was proud to sit by his side and get a hug when lunch was over.

What was it about Russell that attracted me to him so? Besides being kind and funny, and eternally patient with me as a little girl, he radiated God's love to me and to everyone around him. He practiced God's instructions for living in peace with others, for being truthful and kind, and for how to yield to God's leading in our lives. Russell's wife had health struggles and passed away while I was in college. But he never left her side, and never treated her with anything but love and respect. He lived many more years after her passing, and long after his hair was gray and he walked slowly and painfully, his life still radiated with God's love and presence. More than 60 years have passed since I first met him, but his influence remains.

I'm one of the older ones now, with gray hair and limited physical abilities of my own. I can only hope that others can see God radiating through me the way I could with Russell. I pray that someday someone will say "I saw God in her life, and my life is different because of it."

Prayer: Dear God, thank you for Russell and other men and women like him who have had an impact on me over the years. Help me to be an influence in the world to those who are younger. I want to reflect your love, today and always. Amen.

Application:

_____

_____

_____

_____

_____

_____

CHAPTER 37

Words

Today's Scripture: Proverbs 18:21
"Words kill, words give life; they are
either poison or fruit – you choose."

Reflection: "Betty, Betty, Betty… Just how stupid are you anyway?" The voice on the other end of the phone was the president of the company where I worked, and I felt myself sink into my chair. Once again, he was belittling me and treating me like the scum of the earth. As a young single mother, I really needed this job, but the daily harassment was almost more than I could stand. His words were killing me, a little bit every day. Eventually my situation changed, and I was able to start work with a different employer. It wasn't long before I felt like a giant weight had been lifted from my shoulders and everyone (from the CEO on down) treated me with kindness and respect. Words of friendship and acceptance were shared between employees, and also when dealing with our customers. Many of my coworkers had been there for 20-30 or more years, and I certainly could understand why. The atmosphere was no longer poisoned with hostility and fear but filled with the sweet fragrance of respect and trust.

Many years have passed since then, but that memory remains fresh for me and serves as a reminder to choose my words carefully and to be aware of their impact on others. What is my response to clerks at the store or servers in a restaurant when things don't go my way? When I am having a bad day, do I snap at the person ahead of me in line, or at my family when I finally get home from work, even though they are just innocent bystanders? Do I see how my words impact those around me, especially those who are younger or more vulnerable? Is the poison on my lips an outward sign of the poison in my heart?

Prayer: Dear Father, thank you for your Word that teaches us how to live more fruitful lives. Help me to watch my words, and to consider the consequences and impact of what I say. I want to reflect your sweet loving nature through my words to others. Let my speech be filled with words of hope, faith, and love. Amen.

Application:

_____

_____

_____

_____

_____

_____

CHAPTER 38

Speak My Name

Today's Scripture: Isaiah 43:1 "But now, thus says the Lord, who created you, Jacob, and formed you, Israel. Do not fear, for I have redeemed you; I have called you by name; you are mine."

Reflection: One of the more challenging things for expectant parents is to decide on a name for their newborn. Many different factors go into selecting just the right name – whether it includes a family ancestor, or they want to select something common but not overly trendy. Everyone around them seems to have an opinion, and the pressure to do it right is high. Baby Name books are popular, and hours are spent deciding on just the right one. The nursery may be decorated with the chosen name, or embroidered blankets may appear at the baby shower. The baby will soon learn to recognize their name and respond to their parents' voices. Most parents usually take this responsibility very seriously.

We all love to hear our name spoken – it is confirmation that we are recognized by others. We are not an anonymous face lost in a crowd, but a real person with an identity. When spoken with love by someone we care about, there is nothing sweeter than our name – we feel valued and included.

There have been billions of people on earth since creation, but God knows each one of us and calls each of us by our name. We are important to him, and he wants us to live with him forever. He knows each one of us personally, and our name is like honey on his lips. Nothing is sweeter than hearing him call my name, speaking to me words of love and forgiveness. He calls my name, and I am his.

Prayer: Dear Father, thank you for loving me and knowing my name. Even if there is someone with my identical name, you know ME. You have redeemed me to live with you in heaven forever, and I belong to you. Amen.

Application:

_____

_____

_____

_____

_____

_____

CHAPTER 39

Good Medicine

Today's Scripture: Proverbs 17:22 "A merry heart does good like medicine."

Reflection: I'll be the first to admit, I don't make a very good patient when I am sick. Mostly, I just want to be left alone and to take the medicine I know will help me feel better. But at the same time, I want someone around to check on me and show they care. When I was young, I was plagued with frequent throat infections and missed many days of school each year. My mother was a nurse and could recognize my symptoms easily, but our family doctor never believed her and insisted that I go to his office so he could look at my tonsils and say "yes, it's her throat again, here is the usual medicine." After just a few doses, I would be feeling better and begging to go back to school. The proper medicine was all I needed.

It's the same way when you share a cheerful smile or friendly word with others. How many times has your spirit been lifted by a kind word from a stranger or someone holding the door for you when your arms were full of packages? Do you know someone who always seems to be positive and cheerful? I had a friend Mary Jo who was someone I could count on to cheer me up when I was low. She listened patiently, but more than that, she just seemed to know the right things to say to help me feel better. Her merry heart was good for my soul.

Prayer: Dear Father, thank you for the people you have put in my life to cheer me up when I am down and to refresh my weary soul. Help me to be that type of person to those around me. Amen.

Application:

_____

_____

_____

_____

_____

_____

CHAPTER 40

Ethics

Today's Scripture: Colossians 3:23
"Whatever you do, work heartily as
for the Lord and not for men."

Reflection: Ethics is described as what you do when no one is watching. I remember as a child being asked to clean my room – not my favorite task. I would procrastinate as long as possible and then kick things under my bed or shove them to the back of the closet. I thought I was getting away with it by taking the easy way out, but somehow my mom always knew. In later years, I had a job 'walking beans.' For those of you who don't know, it involved walking up and down row after row after row of soybean plants and pulling weeds by hand. It was hot and dirty and back-breaking work, but it paid well. We were supposed to pull ALL of the weeds, but I will admit there were times that I skipped a few (or more than a few) weeds because I was too hot and tired, and my hands were filled with blisters. I figured if the weeds were small, the farmer would not notice, and I could go home and rest. But I imagine it was obvious within a day or two once they grew bigger.

It took until I was an adult to understand that just because I was not being watched by my mom or a boss, God was watching, and I was being disrespectful. God sees all my efforts, and doing my best for him should be a top priority, whether others are aware of it or not. My current employment involves working from home. It would be easy to find ways to not work while on the clock: playing games on my phone, watching TV, or even taking a nap. But my desire is to do my best work always – both for my employer and for God.

Prayer: Dear God, whatever task I am assigned, please help me to see that delighting you is the most important thing. Yes, I want my family and my employer to be pleased, but nothing is more essential than doing my best for you. Amen.

Application:

_____

_____

_____

_____

_____

_____

CHAPTER 41

Where is Your Treasure?

Today's Scripture: Luke 12:34
"For where your treasure is, there
your heart will be also."

Reflection: According to family folklore, I am the 4th cousin of Jesse James the bank robber. I was told that my great grandmother Rosa James' father was Jesse's father's brother. She told stories to my grandmother about times that Jesse was being chased by a posse and they hid him in their barn. I wrote a book report about him when I was in high school and have continued to learn more about him over the years. One of the more interesting stories is that after a train robbery in Gad's Hill, Missouri, Jesse buried a large sum of money in the Ozark hills. Countless searches have been done by treasure hunters who have spent thousands of hours looking for the lost riches. The exact value of the treasure is not known, but it was large enough to make Jesse want to hide it and large enough to inspire hundreds of people to search for it.

I've thought a lot about Jesse over the years, and wondered why he would go to such extremes, including shooting people, for a few bags of gold coins or cash. But before I can be too critical of him, I have to ask myself what my treasure is. I am an avid paper crafter, and love making and selling greeting cards. And based on the overflowing condition of my craft room, buying papers and inks may be a 'treasure' to me. But is it really the best use of my time and money? Sure, my cards help to spread caring thoughts and sympathy across the country, but do I desire to spend more time making cards than I do reading my Bible and memorizing scripture, talking about God with my neighbors, or fostering relationships with friends and family? Where does my treasure truly lie?

Prayer: Dear Father, thank you for giving us talents and interests in creative areas such as art or music or gardening. But help me to ultimately keep my eyes on you, as the author and finisher of my faith. I can use my talents and gifts for you, of course, but the focus needs to remain on you and not on what I am able to accomplish. Forgive me for the times I have been more interested in what I can make rather than the beautiful world that you have already made for me to enjoy. Thank you for loving me. Amen.

Application:

_____

_____

_____

_____

_____

_____

CHAPTER 42

Taking it for Granted

Today's Scripture: Ephesians 1:3-4
"Blessed be the God and Father of our
Lord Jesus Christ, who has blessed
us with every spiritual blessing in the
heavenly places in Christ, just as He
chose us in Him before the foundation
of the world, that we should be holy and
without blame before Him in love."

Reflection: The alarm rings and you stretch as you get out of bed. You turn on the light and head to the bathroom for a quick shower. The cat is pestering you because she wants to be fed, so you feed her and then fix breakfast for yourself – maybe something from the fridge or microwave. You take a roast out of the freezer and put it in the crockpot for dinner tonight. Soon you walk into your home office, turn on your computer, and begin your day. It doesn't matter how cold or hot it is outside, you are comfortable. After work you watch tv or YouTube videos while fixing dinner, then do a load of laundry or vacuum the living room. All of these things are brought to you by electricity and internet – two things that are easy to take for granted. I know I did. That is, until June 18, 2023, at about midnight when my town was struck with 100 mph winds causing massive damage and power outages across the city. I am writing this a few days later while sitting at a cooling station, still several days away from getting power back. Oh, and the heat index is over 100 degrees! My house is dark and hot, and my cat and I are truly suffering. How I wish I could just flip a switch and have things go back to normal!

During this crisis, I've done a lot of thinking about taking things for granted. Our verse above says God has blessed us with every spiritual blessing– how often do I thank him for that? I expect him to be available whenever I have a problem, or when I take the time to open my Bible or attend church. Christianity and worship are on my schedule, whenever it's convenient. He has done so much for me, and I do not appreciate it as I should. I vow to do better from here on.

Prayer: Thank you, Father – sometimes that is all I can say. I am so sorry that I have taken your love and salvation for granted, expecting you to be available whenever the mood strikes me. Please forgive me for my selfishness and help me to choose you above all else. Amen.

Application:

_____

_____

_____

_____

_____

_____

CHAPTER 43

God's Handiwork

Today's Scripture: Ephesians 2:10 "For
we are God's handiwork, created in
Christ Jesus to do good works, which
God prepared in advance for us to do."

Reflection: I never considered myself to be an overly
creative person. I cannot draw or paint – even my
stick people look like they need surgery! I have
tried lots of crafts over the years – sewing, cross-
stitch, candle making, baking, etc., but never was
overly pleased with the results. Several years ago, I
started scrapbooking, which quickly bored me, but it
opened the world of card making to me. I look back
now at my earliest attempts, and wow, have I come
a long way. I have made thousands of cards over the
years, but what brings me the most joy is when I give
them away to charities or as gifts to friends and family at Christmas. During the COVID pandemic, I
made literally hundreds of 'thinking of you' cards for

people to send to their loved ones. My mother was locked in her nursing facility for about 18 months, and the cards she was able to send were her main communication to family and friends. My cards are not the most elaborate or fancy, but they are a way for me to help spread God's love to others. I am so glad that I started practicing early and had supplies and the confidence to fill this need when the time came.

Do you know what gift God has given you? What are you doing with it? More than just a talent, God has given you a gift that is meant to be shared with others, and to do good works in the world. It doesn't have to be big or fancy – you probably won't win awards or get rich. Your gift just needs to be shared with others to show God's love and salvation.

Prayer: Dear God, help me to recognize the gifts you have so generously given me. Help me to cultivate those gifts and to look for ways to share with others. You created me for good works, and I do not want to shy away from using what you gave me. Amen.

Application:

_____

_____

_____

_____

_____

_____

CHAPTER 44

The Fortress

Today's Scripture: Psalm 62:6-8 "Truly
he is my rock and my salvation; he is my
fortress; I will not be shaken. My salvation
and my honor depend on God; he is my
mighty rock, my refuge. Trust in him
at all times, you people; pour out your
hearts to him, for God is our refuge."

Reflection: Like most kids, my friends and I used to play tag at recess during school. One person was selected as 'it' and the rest of us ran around trying not to get caught. If the person who was 'it' caught me, he would say "Tag, you're it!" and it was my turn to chase others. I never was the fastest runner, so I got tagged fairly often. But the one thing that would save me was when I could reach our base (usually the tether ball pole or some other piece of playground equipment). Many times, I was out of breath and barely able to make it, but I knew if I could just touch the base, I would be safe. There was no other way – until the whistle blew and recess was over, my only security was clinging to the base.

God is our safe place – our refuge in times of trouble. When things are tough and the challenges of life are chasing us, there is no other place or thing that offers us the security we need. It is not found in others, in material things or in a big bank account. There were other pieces of playground equipment where I could try to hide, but none of them was sufficient to save me. God alone is where we are to place our faith and trust.

Prayer: Dear God, help me to run to you in times of trouble. Any efforts I make on my own may hide me for a while, but ultimately it is only when I am safe in your shelter that I am protected. Thank you for loving me, and for giving me a way of escape from the trials of this life. Amen.

Application:

_____

_____

_____

_____

_____

_____

CHAPTER 45

Cry For Help

Today's Scripture: Psalm 119:147
"I rise before dawn and cry for
help; I hope in your words."

Reflection: I start work at 6 AM, so my alarm is set for 5. Because I work from home, I don't need to worry about getting dressed up or commuting. I have a rescue cat named Molly, who is very quirky and demanding. She has not learned to read a clock, of course, and insists that 3:30 AM is the correct time to wake me up and for me to feed her. She will sit by my bed and 'talk' to me, but when that does not get the results she wants, she will run and jump on me, or dive onto me from the headboard. She continues to cry and bug me until I finally give up and feed her. It doesn't matter how much food is already in her bowl – if she can see the bottom, she freaks out. Of course, by now we are both awake and she thinks it's playtime. I can be known to be a bit grumpy during this daily routine, wishing she could figure out how to wait a while for breakfast. Before long, it's 5 AM and my alarm goes off, and I must get up for real to get ready for the day.

How many times have I been awake in the middle of the night and worried about a problem? I get burdened with family situations, health issues, financial concerns, fears of the future – and have been on my knees crying to God for guidance and for a way through the difficult times. My hope is in him, and he does not care whether it is day or night. He doesn't tell me it's too early, or to learn how to read a clock – and he doesn't care that my food bowl (the Bible) is already overflowing with truth and love. He patiently listens to my cries and wraps his arms around me, comforting me with words of love and hope.

Prayer: Dear Heavenly Father, thank you for always being available when I need you – whether it is 3 AM or 3 PM or anywhere in between. Help me to show the same consideration and compassion to others, whether human or feline. Amen.

Application:

_____

_____

_____

_____

_____

_____

CHAPTER 46

Peace

Today's Scripture: Romans 5:1
"Therefore, since we have been justified
through faith, we have peace with God
through our Lord Jesus Christ."

Reflection: Whenever we see the word 'therefore,' we should look back a few verses to see what it is 'there for.' The final verse of chapter 4 states "He was delivered over to death for our sins and was raised to life for our justification." We are justified before God because of the sacrifice and death of Jesus. It is not through anything we can do on our own - not by attending church, memorizing scripture, doing good works, or giving large sums of money. It doesn't matter who our parents are or if our ancestors were founding members of the church. Our peace with God comes only by believing in God's love for us and personally accepting him as our savior in faith. But once we do, he gives us peace during difficult times: health issues, job loss, financial stresses, or in the midst of our unsettled world. We are not promised a life without challenges, but he does promise to stay with us and give us his comfort and peace.

Are you taking full advantage of this peace, or are you struggling alone, trying to do things on your own? Do we feel that you are doing 'good works' and that is all that is required? Call out to him today, asking him to give you his peace. God is good, all the time. And all the time, God is good.

Prayer: Dear Father, thank you for your sacrifice and providing for me a way of salvation. I cannot do anything on my own that would merit your favor. Help me to share this story of reconciliation and peace with others. Amen.

Application:

_____

_____

_____

_____

_____

_____

CHAPTER 47

I Am Slipping

Today's Scripture: Psalm 94:18 "I cried out, 'I am slipping!' but your unfailing love, O Lord, supported me."

Reflection: I remember trying to learn to ice skate when I was a young girl. The farm where we lived had a small creek along the west side, and the harsh Iowa winters usually ensured that it would freeze solid enough for us to skate. After dad inspected it and was sure it was safe, we would spend most of one afternoon clearing all the snow from the ice. The next day we would bundle up and lace up the skates that mom picked up at Goodwill. My older siblings were good skaters, but my lack of athletic ability was obvious as I struggled to stay upright. I spent a lot of time sitting on the cold ice instead of gliding gracefully like my sisters and older brother could. My dad loved to skate as well, and I remember him coming to me and holding my hand as he patiently taught me the tricks I needed to be successful. Many times, his strong arms caught me as I started to tumble and fall. Eventually my ankles got used to balancing on thin blades, and with the confidence I gained by having my father by my side, I was able to succeed.

God is always there to help us when we fall during life's slippery times - health problems, financial concerns, natural disasters - all we need to do is call to him in faith and he will catch us with his strong arms. Let him support you and guide you while you build your faith and confidence in living for him.

Prayer: Dear Father, thank you for the many times you have caught me as I was slipping on life's dangerous roads. You never take your eyes off me, and I know you will always come when I call. Help me to stay aware of your presence in my life each day. Amen.

Application:

_____
_____
_____
_____
_____
_____

CHAPTER 48

Be Kind

Today's Scripture: Micah 6:8 "Do what is right to other people, love being kind to others, and live humbly."

Reflection: When I was in high school, we lived about three blocks from the school. One cold winter afternoon as I was walking home, I passed the teachers' parking lot where all the cars were covered with several inches of new fluffy snow. My mom was the school nurse, and as I got to her car, I decided to clean it off for her. I opened her car door (we didn't routinely lock our cars in this small town back in the 70's) and found her snow scraper with a brush on the end. I cleaned all the snow off her car, then thought it would be fun to do a few more. Before long, I had brushed off eight or ten cars but was getting cold so decided it was enough. I put the scraper back in my mom's car and then walked the rest of the way home. I wish I could have seen the look on my teachers' faces when they saw their cars cleaned off! After about 30 minutes, my mom came home and told me about the fun surprise of clean cars and wondering who would do such a kind thing? I never did admit it to her but kept it as my little secret. It really was a small thing and only took a few minutes of my time, but it meant a lot to them.

Our verse above reminds us to be kind to each other, to love doing good things. Whether it is paying someone's toll or buying the Starbucks for the car behind you, doing good does not need to be difficult or expensive. Is your neighbor elderly or have health problems and now having trouble keeping the lawn mowed or weeds pulled? Maybe there is a new mom in the neighborhood who would appreciate you running errands or picking up dinner? Open your eyes and look at those around you. What small thing could you do to make their day? And maybe keep it your own little secret – it's fun!

Prayer: Dear Father, open my eyes to see ways to show your love and kindness to others. Help me to be sensitive to the needs of others and to be creative in meeting those needs. Keep me humble, not seeking attention or praise. Amen.

Application:

_____

_____

_____

_____

_____

_____

CHAPTER 49

Worship

Today's Scripture: Psalm 63:3 (Msg) "So
here I am in the place of worship, eyes open,
drinking in your strength and glory. In
your generous love I am really living at last!
My lips brim with praises like fountains.
I bless you every time I take a breath; My
arms wave like banners of praise to you."

Reflection: Differing styles of worship seem to be a common conflict within today's church. Whether by singing traditional hymns or more contemporary songs, everyone seems to worship in a different fashion or volume. Personally, I prefer more traditional hymns and a respectful environment, but I know that is not for everyone. Our verse above doesn't tell us how to worship, just that we should. Whether singing softly or loudly, our lips can still joyfully sing God's praises. And whether my arms are raised toward heaven or folded in my lap, my worship no more or less meaningful or acceptable to him.

Don't let others make you feel uncomfortable worshiping in the way that is most meaningful for you. Sing, clap, and wave your hands if you wish, or close your eyes and let a silent tear of thankfulness slip down your cheek. God sees you and knows what is in your heart. He just wants you to be genuine as you worship him.

Prayer: Dear Father, you are worthy of our praise Help me be more understanding of differing styles and preferences, and not to impress my methods too strongly on others. You see my heart and my love for you. Amen

Application:

_____

_____

_____

_____

_____

_____

CHAPTER 50

You Are There

Today's Scripture: Psalm 139:7-10 "Where can I go from your Spirit? Where can I flee from your presence? If I go up to the heavens, you are there; if I make my bed in the depths, you are there. If I rise on the wings of the dawn, if I settle on the far side of the sea, even there your hand will guide me, your right hand will hold me fast."

Reflection: In 2004 I packed up my belongings and moved from the Midwest to central California. I had a job lined up (a promotion!) and had rented an apartment sight unseen. My daughter rode with me as we drove for two days. We finally arrived in the town of Paso Robles and checked into a hotel for the night. The next morning, I met a property manager who had the apartment key and we drove to my new home. There was a lot of drama with my moving company damaging several of my items and stealing a few others. I had thought God had opened the door for me at this new company, but everything seemed to be going wrong. In a day or two I took my daughter to the airport so she could fly home, and realized I was over 1000 miles away from any member of my family, for the first time in my life. I was lonely and homesick. Maybe I had made a mistake? Was this really what God had wanted?

One Sunday afternoon I was restless, so I got in my car and drove to the coast – about one half hour away. I found a spot that had a place to park and a single picnic table. No one else was there, and I felt I had the whole ocean to myself. I sat there with my eyes closed, listening to the waves and seagulls, and feeling the warm sunshine on my face. It wasn't long before I felt God's presence and the calming of my spirit. He knew where I was and knew the plans he had for me. I sat there until the sunset reflected gold and orange on the water. I knew God loved me, whether I lived in California or Oklahoma or Maryland, or anywhere in between.

Prayer: Thank you, God, for loving me and keeping an eye on me, wherever I wander. You know when things are going well, and when I am struggling. You see when I am surrounded by friends or when I am far from home and lonely. Help me feel your closeness whether I am alone or in a crowd. Amen.

Application:

_____

_____

_____

_____

_____

_____

CHAPTER 51

God's Armor

Today's Scripture: Ephesians 6:10-11
"Finally, be strong in the Lord and in the strength of his might. Put on the whole armor of God, that you may be able to stand against the schemes of the devil."

Reflection: Many years ago, I was employed at a company that treated its workers very poorly. It was a hostile environment, and most everyone was depressed and looking to escape. I was a young single mother and really needed this job, even though it crushed my spirit, and I cried each day as I forced myself to go. I was totally weighed down by negative feelings. The devil wanted me to be depressed and discouraged, ultimately defeated. Later in life I learned how I could have been better prepared for this battle by studying God's word. We have the choice of how we dress each day, and the scriptures above give us excellent advice. These verses show us where to start, and the following few verses (12-17) explain how each part of this armor will help fight the negative thoughts we all have at times.

Belt of Truth – First, we are to pick up the belt of truth which wraps completely around us and surrounds us with God's promises. Time spent in Bible study and memorization, along with prayers of surrender and for guidance, would have started my day with a more positive attitude and helped me focus on God instead of my difficult situation.

Breastplate of Righteousness – Secondly, we are to cover our heart (emotions) with a breastplate which will serve as our main protection against the darts of negativity the devil aims in our direction. My emotions needed protection during this difficult time, and I wish I had asked for help putting on God's breastplate.

Shoes of Peace – Next, we are to put on the shoes of the preparation of the gospel of peace. God's shoes protect our feet from figurative rocks and glass on the road, not only as we fight our battle against evil, but also as we go into the world and share the good news of God's deliverance in our lives.

Shield of Faith – Even if we have the best armor, the devil will continue to fling arrows at us, looking for small weaknesses. These are arrows of self-doubt, discouragement, anxiety, and depression. I needed God's shield of faith to protect me from the evil one.

Helmet of Salvation – Our armor would not be complete without a helmet to protect our head (thoughts) from negativity. I was bombarded daily by hateful words from my supervisor and co-workers. I needed this protection not just in my work environment but also negative influences from various sources – social media and tv, toxic relationships, and even my friends and family.

Sword of the Spirit – Lastly, we are to pick up our sword which is the word of God. Scripture memorization is key here and would have helped me go on the offensive to fight back against the enemy.

Prayer: Dear Father, thank you for the Bible that describes the armor that shields and protects me, and for giving me the ability to fight back when needed. Discouraging thoughts and emotions surround me every day, but there is no need for me to fight them alone. Remind me to stay near to you, and to willingly accept the tools you have given me to fight against the negative forces of the devil. Help me to rely on you, and to share the good news of your love with others. I need you by my side, always. I love you. Amen.

Application:

_____
_____
_____
_____
_____
_____

CHAPTER 52

Shame

Today's Scripture: Psalm 34:4-5 "I
sought the Lord and he answered me;
he delivered me from all my fears. Those
who look to him are radiant, their
faces are never covered with shame."

Reflection: Shame is defined as a painful emotion resulting from an awareness of inadequacy or guilt. It is so painful that we often try to hide from our failure being found out, and then hang our heads when confronted. It is almost impossible to look into the eyes of our friends or family when we know our actions have hurt them. I think we have all seen pictures of dogs who have totally destroyed a sofa or a child who has spilled paint all over the carpet. Their faces are downcast, and they are unable to make eye contact. Recently, my granddaughter intentionally disobeyed an instruction her mother gave her about not using an expensive painting set without supervision. She did it anyway, and when she was caught, she refused to admit she was wrong even while hanging her head in shame. Her stubbornness and impulsiveness to not wait for help and refusal to take the blame for her actions resulted in punishment and hurt feelings. How much better it would have been if she had just admitted what she did wrong and asked for forgiveness!

God offers relief from our shame if we will lift our faces and look to him. Ask him and he will deliver you, and your downcast eyes and tears will be replaced with a radiant glow of faith and peace.

Prayer: Dear Father, thank you that I can come to you without fear and shame – you rescue me, forgive me, and fill me with your peace. My face is radiant as I look into your loving eyes and feel your love and acceptance. Amen.

Application:

_____

_____

_____

_____

_____

_____

CHAPTER 53

I Will Remember (Leap Year)

Today's Scripture: Psalm 77:11-12 "I will
remember the deeds of the Lord;
yes, I will remember your wonders of old. I
will ponder all your work,
and meditate on your mighty deeds."

Reflection: When I first considered writing devotionals that would include personal stories, I wasn't sure I had enough memories that would be appropriate. I am just a simple Iowa farm girl who has moved around a lot as an adult and spent most of my working career in healthcare. Did I really have anything special to say that others would find meaningful and uplifting? Could my simple stories be used to lead others to a deeper relationship with God? Once I started writing, what I experienced was the opposite of what I feared—I would read a scripture and close my eyes, asking God to free my mind and bring the appropriate memories back to me. After a few deep breaths, suddenly I was transported back to my farm, my college dorm, or my apartment in California. I was talking to my grandparents again, singing in church or praying for forgiveness. Sometimes it was a snowy blizzard, but other times it was a bright sunny spring day. Memories of sights and sounds and smells came flooding back, along with the peace of knowing that God was with me through it all. Reliving these experiences confirmed to me that I was never alone, that God's love was with me from my earliest memories, and that I was blessed to have been surrounded by parents, pastors and friends who guided me and pointed me to the path of godly living. Yes, I fell off that path many times and often hurt myself badly, but God was always there to help me up, brush me off, and set me back on the path again. Memories of these crashes were painful, but I still smile, knowing God was always by my side.

Prayer: Dear God, thank you for bringing these memories back to me, and whether they were sweet or painful, thank you for always being there with me. Help me to be more aware each day of your presence in my life, and to be more open in sharing your faithfulness to me with others. Amen.

Application:

_____

_____

_____

_____

_____

_____

Final Thoughts

Thank you for spending these past 53 weeks with me as we reflected on God's character and discovered ways we can be more like him. It has been my pleasure to share my memories and the teachings of my parents and others who shaped me. My prayer is that you found them enjoyable to read and relatable to situations in your own life.

It is also my hope that these short devotionals have helped start a habit of weekly Bible reading or have supplemented the other readings you already do. Please find time to memorize the verses that mean the most to you – I'm so thankful for the times God gives a verse back to me just when I need it.

May God richly bless you in the years to come.

Betty Gossell